RED BIRD SINGS

The Story of *Zitkala-Ša,*
Native American Author, Musician, and Activist

Adapted by
GINA CAPALDI & Q. L. PEARCE
Illustrations by GINA CAPALDI

CAROLRHODA BOOKS
MINNEAPOLIS

For Maia, Zac, and
Oliver who are growing up
in a more enlightened age
—JER

For my daughter Kaitlyn
and my beloved nieces,
Perrie and Jillian.
May their lives be filled
with music and may their
dreams have wings.
—QLP

To my nieces, Annie and
Veronica, who always
bring their sweet smiles
and intelligence
—GC

The images in this book are used with the permission of: Sheet music for *Sundance Opera* by Zitkala-Ša and William F. Hanson, William F. Hanson papers, MSS299, L. Tom Perry Special Collections, Harold B. Lee Library, Brigham Young University, Provo, Utah (LTPSC HBLL BYU), pp. ii (left), 26 (right); Permission granted by the *Atlantic Monthly Magazine*. Masthead revised for artistic purposes, pp. i (right), 5, 29; Courtesy of the author, pp. 10, 16, 18, 21, 24, 25, 29 (left); *Wabash Plain Dealer*, Monday 1 July 1895, courtesy of Indiana State Library, Indiana Division, p. 17; *The Washington Post*, March 17 1900, p. 22; Pamphlet for *Sundance Opera* by Zitkala-Ša and William F Hanson, Raymond and Gertrude Bonnin papers, LTPSC HBLL BYU, p. 26 (left); Letter from Senator Lynn J. Frazier to Gertrude Bonnin. Washington, D.C., 10 March 1927, Raymond and Gertrude Bonnin papers, MSS1704, LTPSC HBLL BYU, p. 28; Letter from President Gertrude Bonnin, NCAI, to Mr. Sniffen, Washington, D.C., 31 March 1927, Raymond and Gertrude Bonnin papers, MSS1704, LTPSC HLBB, BYU, p. 28; Used by permission, Uintah County Library Regional History Center, all rights reserved, p. 30; *Zitkala-Ša* [1898]. Platinum print, 7 3/4 x 5 3/8". Division of Photographic History, National Museum of American History, Smithsonian Institution, Washington, D.C., p. 30.

Cover art © 2011 by Gina Capaldi. Back cover: *Sundance Opera* by Zitkala-Ša and William F Hanson, William F Hanson papers, MSS299, LTPSC HBLL BYU.

Carolrhoda Books
A division of Lerner Publishing Group, Inc.
241 First Avenue North
Minneapolis, MN 55401 USA

For reading levels and more information, look up this title at www.lernerbooks.com.

Library of Congress Cataloging-in-Publication Data

Capaldi, Gina
    Red Bird sings : the story of Zitkala-Ša, Native American author, musician, and activist / by Gina
Capaldi & Q. L. Pearce; illustrated by Gina Capaldi.
        p.   cm.
    Includes bibliographical references.
    ISBN 978–0–7613–5257–0 (lib. bdg. : alk. paper)
    ISBN 978–0–7613–7159–5 (eBook)
    1. Zitkala-Ša, 1876-1938—Juvenile literature. 2. Yankton women—Biography—Juvenile literature.
3. Yankton Indians—Biography—Juvenile literature. 4. Indian women authors—Biography—Juvenile
literature. 5. Indian women activists—Biography—Juvenile literature. 6. Political activists—United
States—Biography—Juvenile literature. 7. Indian musicians—Biography—Juvenile literature. 8. Women
musicians—United States—Biography—Juvenile literature. I. Pearce, Q. L. (Querida Lee) II. Title.
E99.Y25Z53 2011
978.004'975243—dc22   2011003014

Manufactured in the United States of America
4-50256-10904-2/4/2021

AUTHOR'S NOTE

*This book is a tribute to Zitkala-Ša, a remarkable woman
who truly lived in two worlds.*

1876 was the year of the battle at Little Bighorn, or Greasy Grass.
It was an era of westward expansion and the discovery of gold. It
was also a time when American Indian tribal rights were commonly
ignored by the United States government. American Indian
assimilation into the Anglo world was an accepted practice. Indian
children were taken from their families and sent to boarding schools
to be stripped of their language, culture, and spirituality. It is in this
time that Zitkala-Ša's story begins. She was born Gertrude Simmons
on the Yankton Sioux reservation in South Dakota.

As the adapters of this life story, our goal has been to maintain
the spirit and to celebrate the life and achievements of Gertrude
Simmons Bonnin—Zitkala-Ša—American Indian, writer, musician,
and activist. To paint her story we have adapted three serialized
semiautobiographical stories she wrote for the *Atlantic Monthly* in the
early 1900s. They are *Impressions of an Indian Childhood, The School
Days of an Indian Girl,* and *An Indian Teacher Among Indians.*
Beginning with Zitkala-Ša's own words, we have woven additional
primary and secondary sources into the text. We have reworked her
language and substituted modern phrasing for clarity.

The ATLANTIC MONTHLY 1900

The DAY I LOST MY SPIRIT

1884

I remember the day I lost my spirit. It was not the day that the missionaries came to our Indian village to take me and my friends to their eastern boarding school. Nor was it the night that we reached the school grounds where my body trembled more from fear than from the snow I trod upon. It was late the next morning when my friend Judéwin overheard talk of cutting our long, heavy hair.

"No, I will not submit! I will struggle first!" I said.

I crept up the stairs as quietly as I could in my new squeaking shoes. I found a large room with three white beds and crawled under the one in the darkest corner. Loud voices called my name and women entered the room. I watched them open closet doors and peep behind large trunks. Someone threw up the curtains and the room filled with light. I remember being dragged out kicking and scratching. They carried me down the stairs and tied me fast in a chair. I cried and shook my head wildly until I felt the cold blades of the scissors against my neck. Then my keepers gnawed off my thick braids and cut my hair in a shingled style that labeled me as a coward.

I lost my spirit that day. I could not know that it would rise again, stronger and wiser for the wounds it had suffered.

GREAT SHADOWS

1883

The seeds of my journey were sown in an earlier season when I was a wild girl of seven—free as the wind and no less spirited than a bounding deer. My overflowing spirit was my mother's pride. She taught me to have no fear save for intruding upon others. Our tipi stood at the base of some hills. A footpath wound its way through long swamp grasses to the edge of the Missouri River.

Many a summer afternoon, a party of four or five of my playmates roamed over the hills with me. We delighted in impersonating our mothers. I remember how we used to exchange our necklaces, beaded belts, and sometimes even our moccasins. We pretended to offer them as gifts to one another.

In the lap of the prairie we sat and told stories of heroic deeds performed by relatives and exclaimed, "Han! Han!" (Yes! Yes!) When we grew tired of our games or stories, we always returned to chasing the great shadows that played among the hills.

The Iron Horse
February 1884

The first turning away from the easy natural flow of my life occurred in early spring. It was in the month of February of my eighth year. My older brother, Dawée, had returned from three years of education in the East. From my playmates I heard that two paleface missionaries from the Land of Red Apples were in our village. They were from that class of white men who wore big hats and carried large hearts. When they came to our house, an interpreter who knew a smattering of my language joined them.

"Mother, ask them if little girls may have all the red apples they want when they go East," I whispered. The interpreter heard me.

"Yes, little girl, and you will have a ride on the iron horse if you go with these good people."

"Mother, say yes!" I pleaded. Before I went to bed, I begged the Great Spirit to make my mother allow me to go with the missionaries. The next morning my brother came for her decision.

"Dawée, tell the missionaries they may take my little daughter. She will need an education when she is grown."

I was happy. Soon I was being drawn away by the white man's horses. But when I looked back and watched the lonely figure of my mother vanish in the distance, a sense of regret settled upon me.

9

The LAND OF RED APPLES
The Days That Followed 1884

There were eight in our party of bronzed children who were going east with the missionaries. We were three young braves, two tall girls, and three small ones— Judéwin, Thowín, and me. On the train, fair women with tottering babies scrutinized us. Large men with heavy bundles in their hands stared. Children hung themselves upon the backs of seats and pointed at our moccasins and blankets. I sank deep into the corner of my seat, eyes downcast. We traveled seven hundred miles to reach White's Manual Labor Institute in Wabash, Indiana. What I remembered best of that ride were the sweetmeats, or candies, that were tossed out by our keepers.

It was night when we reached the school grounds and were led toward an open door. The noisy hurrying of hard shoes upon a bare wooden floor whirring in my ears frightened me, and I began to cry. The Anglos could not understand the cause of my tears and placed me at a table loaded with food. Because of my sobs, I could swallow very little that evening. I was tucked into bed with one of the tall girls. She talked to me in my mother's tongue and soothed me. Many events would follow, which would force me to be brave in a cold, unknown world.

The ROUTINE
1884–1887

We had a routine during our first three years at White's. A loud bell would awaken us at half past six in the morning. We had a short time to jump into our shoes and clothes, and wet our eyes with icy water before a small bell rang. Bounding down the stairs to the assembly room, we were met by a pale Anglo woman with a roll book and pencil in hand. She looked over the rim of her spectacles at each of us as we answered "here" to the calling of our names.

Each day, we marched off to breakfast and said prayers from a religion different from our own. We practiced our vocational training. Girls were shown how to be housekeepers. We sewed clothes and scrubbed the floors. Boys were trained to be farmers. They tended livestock and repaired fences. Then came our schooling. I loved learning how to read and write. They even taught us how to speak well in public. I appeared to have a talent for such things.

After dinner we heard lectures against drinking and gambling. The Quakers told us about the slavery that had existed in our country not so long ago. They talked about equal rights and how women were not given the same opportunities as men. They stressed tolerance for all people and the importance of fighting against injustice. I listened carefully.

Saturdays meant music lessons! My wounded spirit soared like a bird as I practiced the piano and the violin.

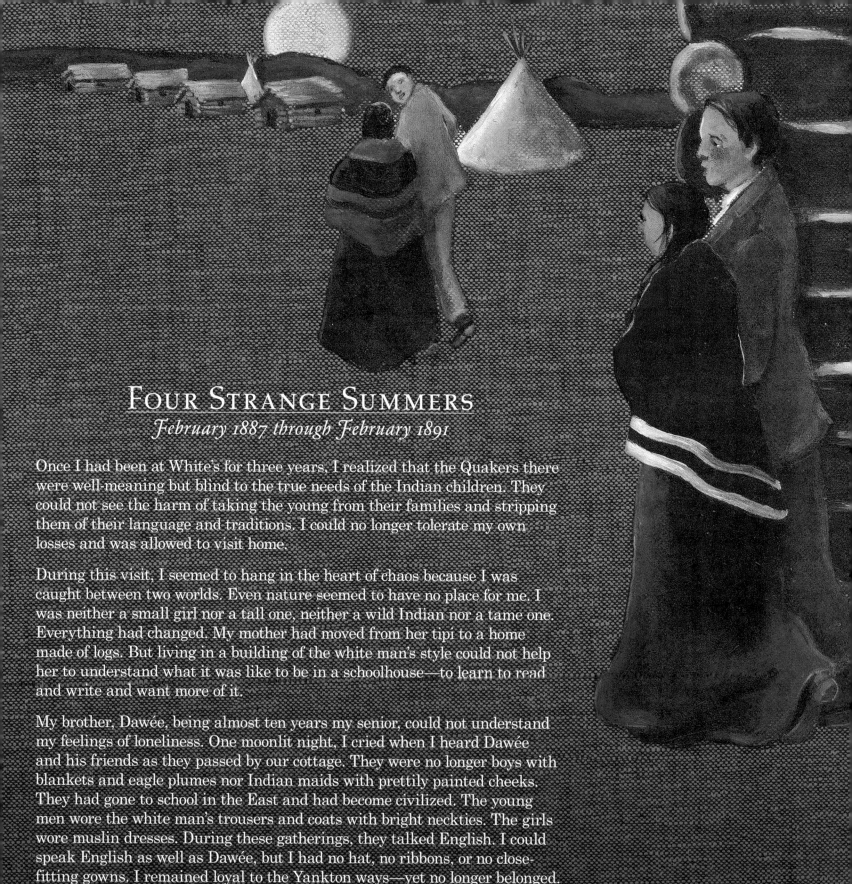

FOUR STRANGE SUMMERS
February 1887 through February 1891

Once I had been at White's for three years, I realized that the Quakers there were well-meaning but blind to the true needs of the Indian children. They could not see the harm of taking the young from their families and stripping them of their language and traditions. I could no longer tolerate my own losses and was allowed to visit home.

During this visit, I seemed to hang in the heart of chaos because I was caught between two worlds. Even nature seemed to have no place for me. I was neither a small girl nor a tall one, neither a wild Indian nor a tame one. Everything had changed. My mother had moved from her tipi to a home made of logs. But living in a building of the white man's style could not help her to understand what it was like to be in a schoolhouse—to learn to read and write and want more of it.

My brother, Dawée, being almost ten years my senior, could not understand my feelings of loneliness. One moonlit night, I cried when I heard Dawée and his friends as they passed by our cottage. They were no longer boys with blankets and eagle plumes nor Indian maids with prettily painted cheeks. They had gone to school in the East and had become civilized. The young men wore the white man's trousers and coats with bright neckties. The girls wore muslin dresses. During these gatherings, they talked English. I could speak English as well as Dawée, but I had no hat, no ribbons, or no close-fitting gowns. I remained loyal to the Yankton ways—yet no longer belonged.

CONTINUING AT WHITE'S MANUAL LABOR INSTITUTE

February 1891 and into 1895

At fifteen, I finally buried the sadness I felt when I first left my mother as a wee child of eight. Books, music, and writing now comforted me. I realized that to have more, I must make my way further into the Anglo world. Against my mother's wishes, I followed my own heart and placed myself into the Quakers hands at White's Institute once more. This time I had a plan, and it was not to become a housekeeper! I loved to learn and was a good student, and I particularly loved the study of music. I had become so accomplished on the violin and the piano that when the music teacher resigned, I was allowed to take her position.

In 1895, I was proud to be presented with my first diploma. During our commencement ceremonies, we recited poetry, sang, and gave speeches. I spoke of the inequality of women. The local newspapers reported that my speech was a "masterpiece that has never been surpassed in eloquence or literary perfection of any girl in this country."

THE DAILY PLAIN DEALER

WABASH, INDIA... ...NDAY EVENING, JULY 1, 1895.

NUMBER 1.

Dr. Charles Little in his evening sermon spoke of the great good accomplished by White's institute, and after showing its boundless works remarked, "But had White's institute accomplished nothing else than the education of this bright, talented girl. Miss Gertrude Simmons, the years of labor would be more than repaid."

Everyone rejoices that Miss Simmons has been afforded the opportunity of attending Earlham college and will go in the fall. She is skilled as a violinist as well as pianist. ...mbition is to educate and cul... ...lf in the highest degree ...n to her own peo... ...r advance...

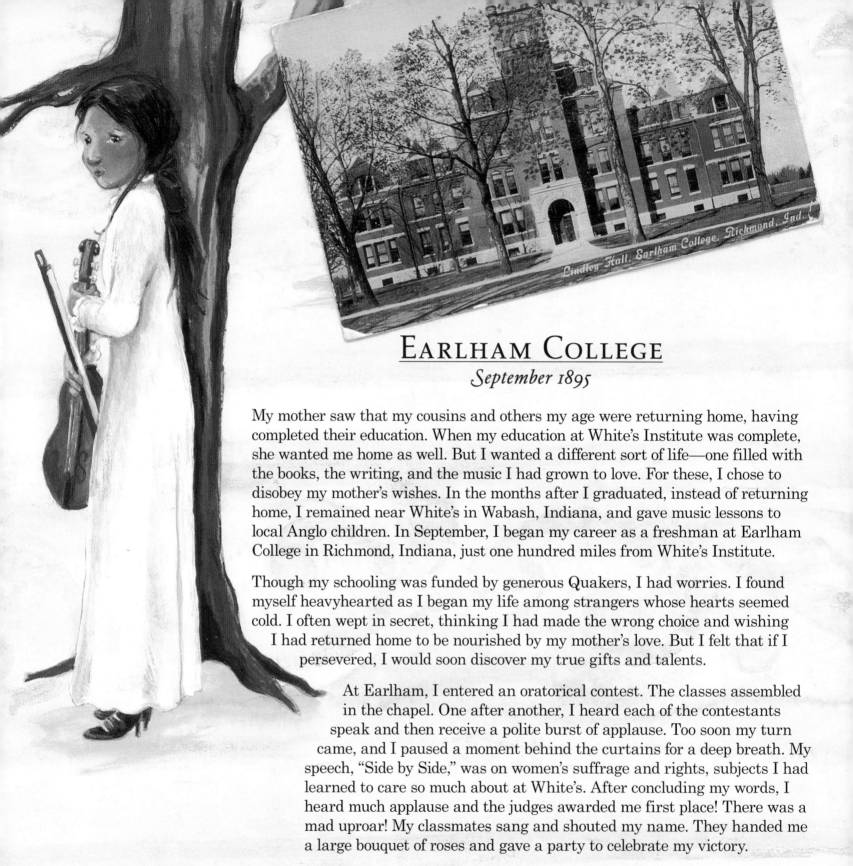

EARLHAM COLLEGE
September 1895

My mother saw that my cousins and others my age were returning home, having completed their education. When my education at White's Institute was complete, she wanted me home as well. But I wanted a different sort of life—one filled with the books, the writing, and the music I had grown to love. For these, I chose to disobey my mother's wishes. In the months after I graduated, instead of returning home, I remained near White's in Wabash, Indiana, and gave music lessons to local Anglo children. In September, I began my career as a freshman at Earlham College in Richmond, Indiana, just one hundred miles from White's Institute.

Though my schooling was funded by generous Quakers, I had worries. I found myself heavyhearted as I began my life among strangers whose hearts seemed cold. I often wept in secret, thinking I had made the wrong choice and wishing I had returned home to be nourished by my mother's love. But I felt that if I persevered, I would soon discover my true gifts and talents.

At Earlham, I entered an oratorical contest. The classes assembled in the chapel. One after another, I heard each of the contestants speak and then receive a polite burst of applause. Too soon my turn came, and I paused a moment behind the curtains for a deep breath. My speech, "Side by Side," was on women's suffrage and rights, subjects I had learned to care so much about at White's. After concluding my words, I heard much applause and the judges awarded me first place! There was a mad uproar! My classmates sang and shouted my name. They handed me a large bouquet of roses and gave a party to celebrate my victory.

I believed then that I had made the right choice.

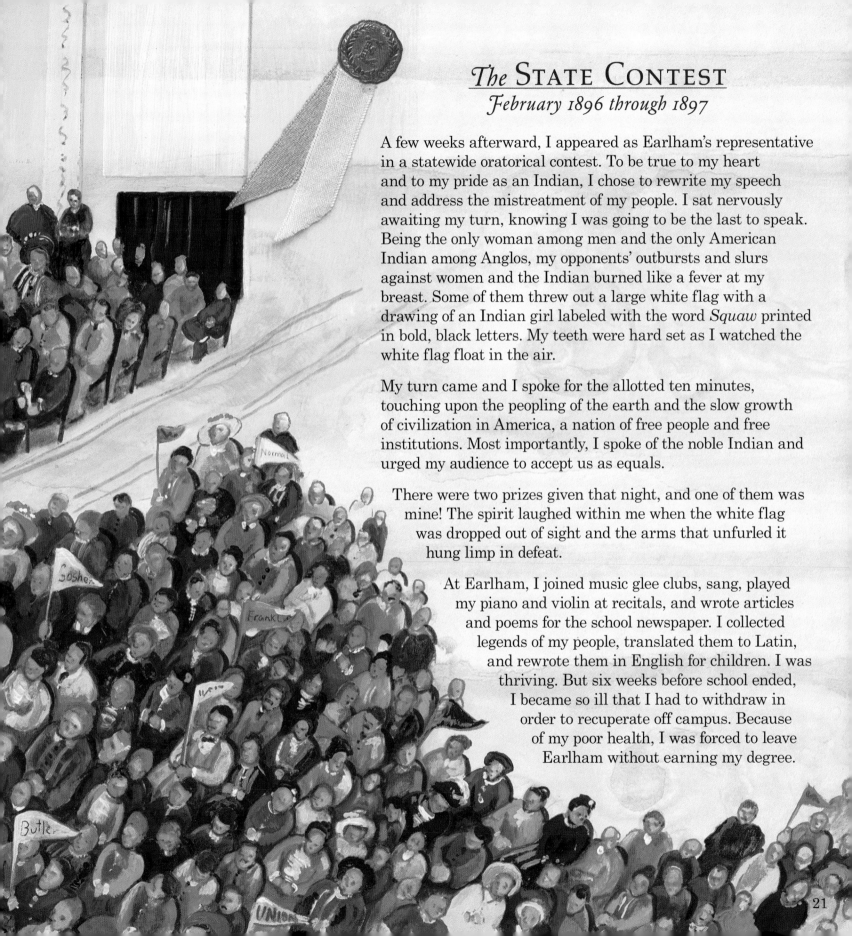

The STATE CONTEST
February 1896 through 1897

A few weeks afterward, I appeared as Earlham's representative in a statewide oratorical contest. To be true to my heart and to my pride as an Indian, I chose to rewrite my speech and address the mistreatment of my people. I sat nervously awaiting my turn, knowing I was going to be the last to speak. Being the only woman among men and the only American Indian among Anglos, my opponents' outbursts and slurs against women and the Indian burned like a fever at my breast. Some of them threw out a large white flag with a drawing of an Indian girl labeled with the word *Squaw* printed in bold, black letters. My teeth were hard set as I watched the white flag float in the air.

My turn came and I spoke for the allotted ten minutes, touching upon the peopling of the earth and the slow growth of civilization in America, a nation of free people and free institutions. Most importantly, I spoke of the noble Indian and urged my audience to accept us as equals.

There were two prizes given that night, and one of them was mine! The spirit laughed within me when the white flag was dropped out of sight and the arms that unfurled it hung limp in defeat.

At Earlham, I joined music glee clubs, sang, played my piano and violin at recitals, and wrote articles and poems for the school newspaper. I collected legends of my people, translated them to Latin, and rewrote them in English for children. I was thriving. But six weeks before school ended, I became so ill that I had to withdraw in order to recuperate off campus. Because of my poor health, I was forced to leave Earlham without earning my degree.

The Washington Post.
WASHINGTON, SATURDAY, MARCH 17, 1900—TWELVE PAGES
CARLISLE INDIAN US SCHOOL
INDIAN BAND CONCERT.
Carlisle Pupils Make Fine Showing and Win Enthusiastic Applause.
One of the surprises of the concert to the audience was a violin solo, Gounod's "Vision de Jeanne d'Arc." The soloist, as announced by the programme, was Zitkala Sa. This musical name proved to belong to a tall, handsomely-formed young Indian maid. As she made her appearance she received round after round of applause from the audience. Miss Zitkala Sa

RED BIRD TAKES WING

July 1897 through 1900

Since my days of my childhood I had been traveling slowly toward the morning horizon. If given the opportunity, I wished to serve as a representative of my people and as an example of what could be accomplished. I accepted an invitation to teach at Carlisle Indian Industrial School in Pennsylvania. There I met Richard Henry Pratt.

"Aha! So you are the little Indian girl who created the excitement among the college orators!" he said. I was anxious to showcase my talents, and Pratt was anxious to see them.

Within my first year at Carlisle, I blossomed. I conducted debates on the treatment of American Indians and gave lectures and dramatic readings. I taught the children music and soon became the leader of the girls' glee club and the pianist for the chapel services.

At Carlisle I was known as the "girl violinist" of its traveling band. We performed with our hearts and souls and took our packed houses by storm. We had the great fortune to play music at the White House, and I read the "Famine" from Longfellow's poem, *Hiawatha*, for President McKinley. When much applause brought me to the stage for a second bow, they presented me with a bouquet of English violets, a moment I will forever cherish.

I had kept my culture in my heart, and now I began to write about it. My stories appeared in the *Atlantic Monthly* in January, February, and March of 1900. I was now known as Zitkala-Ša, Red Bird. Literary societies heartily approved of my work, and the American public was awakened by it. I was encouraged by this and knew that I had many more stories to tell.

PLANTED *in a* STRANGE EARTH

1900–1901

On one early morning, I was summoned to Pratt's office at Carlisle. He was sending me west to gather Indian pupils for the school.

It had been six years since I had been home. As I neared my homeland, I gazed upon the countryside from the train window. The cloud shadows that drifted on the waving yellow of long-dried grasses thrilled me like the meeting of old friends. On the reservation my heart ached when I found my mother's log house in disrepair. The sod roof was trying to spawn tiny sunflowers from the seeds which had been planted by the constant wind.

That night I learned the fate of my brother, Dawée. He had not been able to make use of the education from the eastern school, so he had taken to the plow to feed his wife and two children. I also learned that Anglo settlers had come to live on land promised to our people. An anger surged within me.

I found no way to cool my inflamed feelings. I seemed to be planted in a strange earth that was littered with broken promises to my people. For the white man's books, I had given up my faith in the Great Spirit. For these same books, I had forgotten the healing of trees and brooks. I had let a distance grow between my mother's simple life and my own, and so I had lost her as well.

When I returned to Carlisle in the fall, I prayed to the Great Spirit for direction and a new plan emerged. I became more determined than ever to excel among the Anglos by establishing myself as a musician. I knew that more must be done to improve my talents in order to grow. So I resigned my post at the school to move to Boston in search of creative freedom. For a while, I studied music and voice at the New England Conservatory of Music. But my time in Boston was not long-lived. Yankton called. My family's poverty and my mother's advancing years haunted me.

With a book contract in hand, I went home in 1901 to write the legends of my youth.

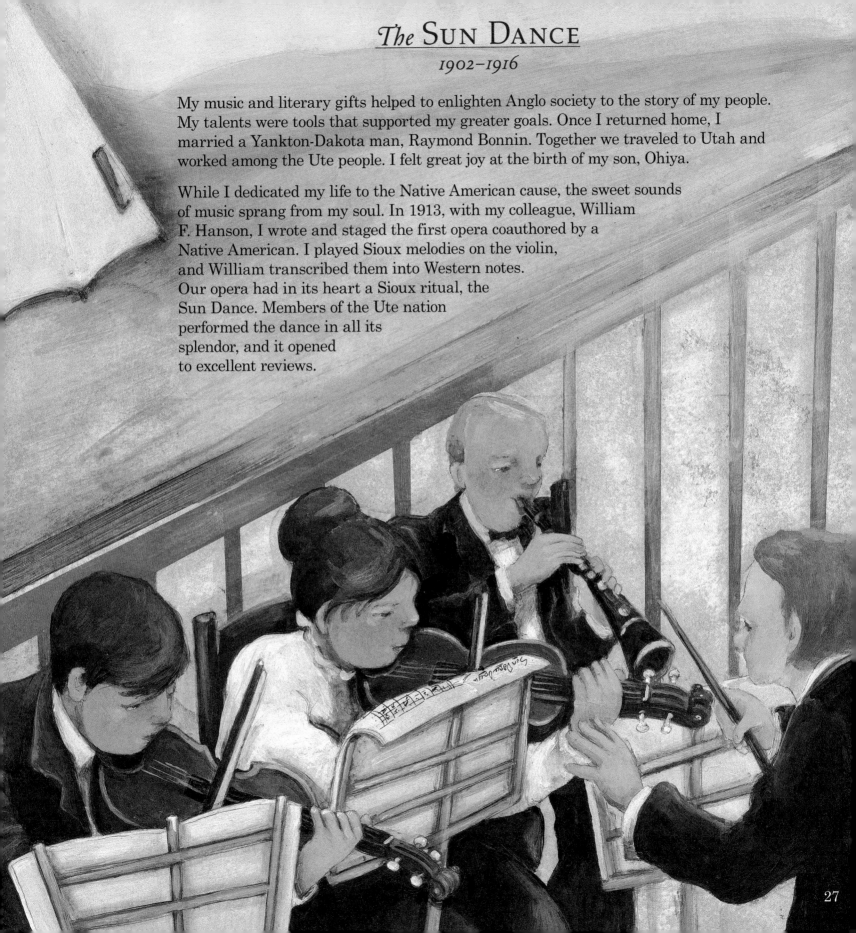

The Sun Dance
1902–1916

My music and literary gifts helped to enlighten Anglo society to the story of my people. My talents were tools that supported my greater goals. Once I returned home, I married a Yankton-Dakota man, Raymond Bonnin. Together we traveled to Utah and worked among the Ute people. I felt great joy at the birth of my son, Ohiya.

While I dedicated my life to the Native American cause, the sweet sounds of music sprang from my soul. In 1913, with my colleague, William F. Hanson, I wrote and staged the first opera coauthored by a Native American. I played Sioux melodies on the violin, and William transcribed them into Western notes. Our opera had in its heart a Sioux ritual, the Sun Dance. Members of the Ute nation performed the dance in all its splendor, and it opened to excellent reviews.

NATIONAL COUNCIL OF AMERICAN INDIANS, Inc.
335 Transportation Building
Washington, D.C.   March 31, 192

Dear brother,-Mrs Sniffen;   This

him if he could innumerate th

Indian situatior

Federa

A. W. HARRELD, OKLA., CHAIRMAN
CHARLES CURTIS, KANS.
CHARLES L. MCNARY, OREG.
LYNN J. FRAZIER, N. DAK.
THOMAS D. SCHALL, MINN.
W. H. MC MASTER, S. DAK.
ROBERT M. LAFOLLETTE, JR., WIS.

HENRY F. ASHURST, ARIZ.
JOHN B. KENDRICK, WYO.
BURTON K. WHEELER, MONT.
C. C. DILL, WASH.
SAM G. BRATTON, N. MEX.

W. T. WARD, CLERK
RAE PINOTTI, ASST. CLERK

United States Senate

COMMITTEE ON INDIAN AFFAIRS

March 10th,

1 9 2 7.

Mrs. Gertrude Bonnim,
735 Transportati
Washi

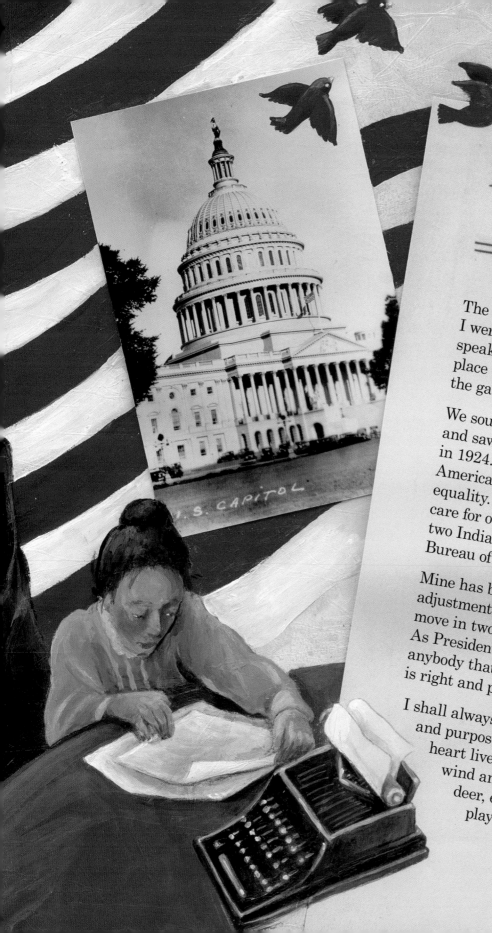

The ATLANTIC MONTHLY

1917–1938

The true course of my life remained. My husband and I were drawn to Washington, D.C., so that we could speak for the rights of the American Indian in the place where policies were made. We quickly learned the game of politics and began to rectify injustices.

We sought the right for Native Americans to vote and saw the passage of the Indian Citizenship Act in 1924. In 1926, we created the National Council of American Indians to continue the fight for rights and equality. We sought improved education and health care for our people and saw President Hoover appoint two Indian Rights Association representatives to the Bureau of Indian Affairs.

Mine has been a life of change and, with it, adjustments. This change gave me the freedom to move in two worlds while never forgetting who I was. As President Lincoln once stated, "I must stand with anybody that stands right; stand with him while he is right and part with him when he goes wrong."

I shall always continue my path as a writer of causes and purposes, a voice for my people. For in my heart lives that wild girl of seven, free as the wind and no less spirited than a bounding deer, ever chasing the great shadows that play among the hills of my home.

Afterword

The melancholy of those black days left so long a shadow that it darkens the path of years that have gone by. Perhaps my Indian nature is the moaning wind which stirs them now for their present record. But, however, tempestuous this is within me, it comes out as a low voice of a curiously colored seashell, which is only for those ears that are bent with compassion to hear it.

—Zitkala-Ša

Gertrude remained frustrated over the treatment of Indians throughout her adult life. She used her gifts with language to transform her literary career to that of political activism. Gertrude became the secretary of the Society of American Indians, whose members worked to improve the lives of Native Americans. She edited the *American Indian* magazine, which tackled issues such as corruption within the Bureau of Indian Affairs and the allotment of tribal lands.

By 1921, Gertrude's most acclaimed literary works were compiled into the book, *The American Indian Stories*, though at least fourteen of her stories would go unpublished until 2001, long after her death.

Gertrude despised inequality regardless of race or sex. In the 1920s she became involved with the General Federation of Women's Clubs (GFWC), an advocacy group dedicated to women's suffrage. Through this organization, Gertrude established the Indian Welfare Committee. With her political influence growing, she was able to investigate and cowrite the article, "Oklahoma's Poor Rich Indians: An Orgy of Graft and Exploitation of the Five Civilized Tribes—Legalized Robbery." Published in 1923, it exposed Anglo corporations that were robbing and murdering Native Americans living on oil land in Oklahoma. Her work was pivotal in moving the government to adopt the Indian Reorganization Act of 1934, which returned management of Indian lands to Native Americans.

(Far left) *Gertrude Simmons holding a violin, 1898*

(Left) *Zitkala-Ša, shown in 1913, often dressed in traditional Indian clothes when she addressed Anglo audiences about the plight of her people.*

In 1926, she founded the National Council of American Indians, an agency that promoted tribal unity to gain political power through citizenship and the vote. She lobbied members of the U.S. Congress to garner support for American Indian issues.

Gertrude Simmons Bonnin broke down barriers. She was the first Native American writer to receive national acclaim; the first Native American violinist to perform before a U.S. president; and the first Native American to write an opera and have it staged. As 'Zitkala-Ša, Red Bird, she celebrated her culture and, at the same time, raised her voice heroically for her people.

She died at the age of sixty-one and, as Gertrude Simmons Bonnin, was buried in Arlington National Cemetery, Washington, D.C. She had taken her place in history as a great American author and a champion for her people.

A Note on the Use of Sources and Materials

This adaptation of Zitkala-Ša's writings in the *Atlantic Monthly* into a picture book format was based on space and pertinence to "story." We paraphrased her language in an effort to clarify it for today's young readers and to emphasize the drama of the day. We encourage readers to explore the breadth and scope of Zitkala-Ša's writings in their original form.

Some scholars suggest that the *Atlantic Monthly* serialized stories are semiautobiographical. Regardless of how closely they reflected her actual life, aspects of what Zitkala-Ša wrote share common themes within the Siouan experiences of the period. To reconstruct the story, we wove in Gertrude's personal information from a variety of sources as listed below. Primary sources and details of Gertrude's life in Utah came from the Papers of Raymond and Gertrude Bonnin housed at the Harold B. Lee Library, Brigham Young University, Provo, Utah.

Selected Bibliography

Carson, Mary Eisenman. *Blackrobe for the Yankton Sioux: Father Sylvester Eisenman, O.S.B. (1891–1948).* Chamberlain, SD: Tipi Press. 1996.

Chiarello, Barbara. "Deflected Missives: Zitkala-Sa's Resistance and Its (Un)Containment." *Studies in American Indian Literatures* 17, no. 3 (Fall 2005): 1–26.

Davidson, Cathy N., and Ada Norris, eds. *Zitkala-Sa: American Indian Stories, Legends, and Other Writings.* New York: Penguin, 2003.

Fisher, Dexter. "Zitkala-Sa: The Evolution of a Writer." *American Indian Magazine,* 5 (1979): 229–238.

Hafen, P. Jane, ed. *Dreams and Thunder: Stories, Poems, and the Sun Dance Opera.* Lincoln: University of Nebraska Press, 2001.

Hamm, Tom. "Side by Side: Zitkala-Sa at Earlham, 1895–1897. From Campus to the Center of American Indian Activism." *Earlhamite,* Winter 1998, 20–22.

Parker, John H., and Ruth Ann Parker. *Josiah White's Institute: The Interpretation and Implementation of His Vision.* Dublin, IN: Prinit Press, 1983.

Picotte, Anges M., and P. Jane Hafen. *Iktomi and the Ducks and Other Sioux Stories.* Lincoln: University of Nebraska Press, 2004.

Spack, Ruth. "Dis/Engagement: Zitkala-Sa's Letters to Carlos Montezuma, 1901–1902." *MELUS* 26, no.1 (2001): 173–204.

Speroff, Leon. *Carlos Montezuma, M.D., The Life and Times of an American Indian, 1866–1923.* Portland, OR: Arnica Publishing, 2003.

Susag, Dorothea M. "Zitkala-Sa (Gertrude Simmons Bonnin); a Power(Full) Literary Voice." *Studies in American Indian Literatures* 5, no. 4 (1993): 3–24.

Welch, Deborah Sue. *Zitkala Sa: An American Indian Leader, 1876–1938.* Ann Arbor, MI: University Microfilms International, 1995.

Partial List of Zitkala-Ša's Writings

Zitkala-Ša. "Impressions of an Indian Childhood." *Atlantic Monthly* 85, no. 507 (January 1900): 37–47.

———. "An Indian Teacher among Indians." *Atlantic Monthly* 85, no. 509 (March 1900): 381–86.

———. "Letter to the Chiefs and Headmen of the Tribes." *American Indian Magazine*, Winter 1919, 196–97.

———. "School Days of an Indian Girl." *Atlantic Monthly Magazine* 85, no. 508 (February 1900): 185–94.

———. "A Soft-Hearted Sioux." *Harper's New Monthly Magazine* 102 (March 1901): 505–509.

———. "The Trial Path." *Harper's New Monthly Magazine* 103 (October 1901): 741–744.

———. "A Warrior's Daughter." *Everybody's Magazine* 6 (April 1902): 346–352.

———. "A Year's Experience in Community Service Work among the Ute Tribe of Indians." *American Indian Magazine*, October–December 1916, 307–310.

Zitkala-Ša, Charles H. Fabens, and Matthew K. Sniffen. "Oklahoma's Poor Rich Indians: An Orgy of Graft and Exploitation of the Five Civilized Tribes—Legalized Robbery." Philadelphia: Office of the Indian Rights Association, 1924.

Further Reading

BOOKS

Campbell, Nicola I. *Shi-shi-etko*. Toronto: Groundwood Books, 2005.

Cerney, Jan. *Images of America: Lakota Sioux Missions, South Dakota*. Charleston, SC: Arcadia Publishing, 2005.

Hoover, T. Herbert. *The Yankton Sioux*. New York: Chelsea House Publishers, 1988.

Levine, Michelle. *The Sioux*. Minneapolis: Lerner Publications Company, 2007.

Littlefield, Holly. *Children of the Indian Boarding Schools*. Minneapolis: Lerner Publications Company, 2001.

National Museum of the American Indian. *Do All Indians Live in Tipis?: Questions and Answers from the National Museum of the American Indian*. New York: HarperCollins, 2007.

Rappaport, Doreen. *The Flight of Red Bird: The Life of Zitkala-Sa*. New York: Puffin Books, 1997.

Reid, Betty, Ben Winton, and Gwendolen Cates. *Keeping Promises: What Is Sovereignty and Other Questions about Indian Country*. Tucson, AZ: Western National Parks Association, 2004.

Zitkala-Sa. *Dance in a Buffalo Skull*. Reprint, Pierre: South Dakota State Historical Society Press, 2007.

———. *Iktomi and the Ducks, and Other Sioux Stories*. Lincoln: University of Nebraska, 1985.

WEBSITES

Arlington National Cemetery Website
http://www.arlingtoncemetery.net/gsbonnin.htm
A biography of Zitkala-Ša is available at this site.

Hanksville, Utah
http://www.hanksville.org/daniel/lakota/Lakota.html
This site offers a brief yet clear description of the three main groups of the Sioux Nation, their bands, dialects, where they settled, and where the tribal lands are located.

Online Archive of Nineteenth-Century U.S. Women's Writings
http://www.facstaff.bucknell.edu/gcarr/19cUSWW/ZS/rh.html
Biographical information on Zitkala-Ša, Gertrude Simmons Bonnin, is available on this site.

Reservation Boarding School System in the United States, 1870–1928
http://www.twofrog.com/rezsch.html
A commentary on the reservations school system and mistreatment of American Indians is provided.

Yankton Sioux Tribe
http://lewisandclarktrail.com/sponsors/yanktonsioux/sect1.htm
This site shows the Yankton Sioux official tribal insignia, its slogan, and its symbolic meaning.

Zitkala Sa (aka Gertrude Simmons) at Carlisle
http://home.epix.net/~landis/zitkalasa
The Carlisle Indian Industrial School newspaper (*Indian Helper*) documented Gertrude Simmons various activities while she was associated with the school.